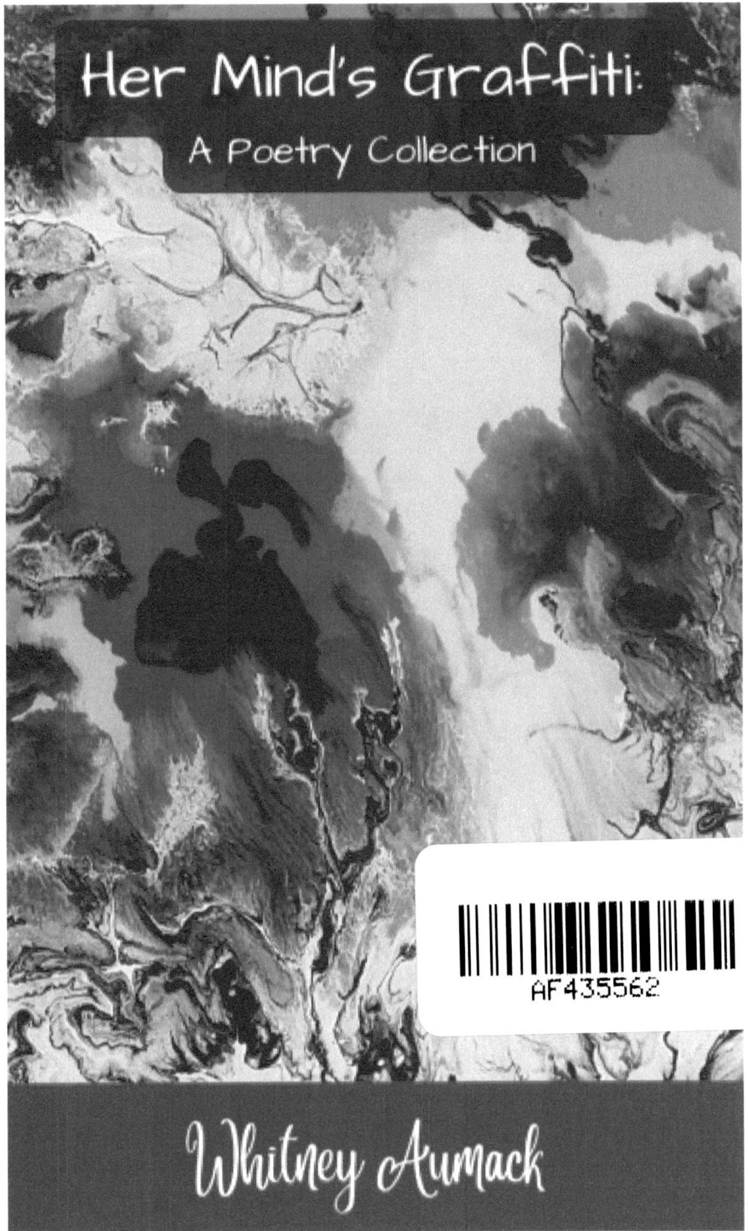
Her Mind's Graffiti:
A Poetry Collection
Whitney Aumack

Her Mind's Graffiti: A Poetry Collection

Her Mind's Graffiti: A Poetry Collection

Aumack, Whitney

ISBN 9798215470947 (Paperback)

Printed and bound in the United States.

Note to the reader: the information is provided for entertainment purposes only.

Dedication

This book is dedicated to those still finding their voice.
I hear you.
XO
W

Welcome

Dear Reader,

I have often wondered whether we would still be beautiful if the thoughts we think everyday were written on our skin. *Her Mind's Graffiti* is my third collection of poetry exposing some of my own deepest thoughts & feelings. Instead of on my skin, I have once again displayed them across the page for all to experience.

I leave it up to you to determine whether those thoughts are beautiful & hopeful or painful & shameful. Whether they are art or vandalism. As always, I leave my work open for your interpretation. Take what you will from it. Feel it. Let it move you. My words are not written to make you comfortable. My words are written to be raw, vulnerable, & crafted in a way that is readable, relatable, & enjoyable to long-time poetry readers, as well as those new to poetry. You will find in all my collections a very unique, personal style and voice that is unlike other contemporary poetry.

Within these pages are poems on love, sex, heartbreak, eating disorder, & everyday life written between 12/2022 and 03/2023.

I am forever grateful for your continued support of my writing adventures. Thank you for choosing *Her Mind's Graffiti.* Thank you for taking a chance on me.

From my pen to your heart,

Whitney Aumack

A skeleton of a miracle

Nerves are frayed
Skin feels flayed
Vulnerable
I ponder the prices I've paid
(Continue to pay)
Sacrifices I've made
(Continue to make)
Making myself uncomfortable
The wars I once waged
With intentions that were honorable
Damage I escaped
Damned me for running away
Alone
From situations that were insufferable
Here I sit
My heart bare as bones
A skeleton of a miracle

Dance in the rain

Come what may
A storm brew inside of me
He said I would dance in the rain if given the chance
I never told him he was my sunshine
Long lost romance still smolders after all this time
He knew a younger me, remembers another me
I'm older now
A little gray
Memories and history
Am I the one who got away
Or is he?
Ten years fly by
We reconnect once more
A nice surprise
I don't want to leave
Until I count the sand on this seashore
Laugh until I cry, it's like no time has passed
If anyone knows me, it's him
Knew. Past tense, past
Take me back to sixteen
Life is different than before
But the other side looks really green
I remember every detail
The texture of his hair
The way his sweater smells

How things taste better when we share
The happiest I've ever been
Was back then with him
And now and again I wish
I had more heart to spare
(Oh, my old friend. You should know I dance in the rain every chance I
get now.)

The Exception

We thought we would be the exception to the rule
Of course
Misery and pain are abstract when it happens to someone else
You may feel the warmth next to the fire, but not the burn
There's a disconnect in our reality
Stand frozen, eyes wide
Fragile humans, life happens to us all
Can you read the future from my palm?
Or decipher the tea leaves from my cup?
I'm not angry, just disappointed
We are not the exception

My rain to your sun

I soared on my imagination into every crevice of your soul
An orange, burning fire where your heart is
I was drawn to its delicate flames
I left a candy trail
Pieces of myself to find the way home
My heavy, rapid heartbeat echoes in the concaves of your mind
I have adapted to the darkness
Inside, outside, the fragmented in between of my conscience
Hardens
Your light is almost too much for me to bear
I navigate the high beam of "could be" and "someday" blindly
Anchored in my own ways, staggering resilience
My rain to your sun, we make rainbows come to life
Blessed stillness
Paint me into your picture, smiling

It reminds me of

We lay on fresh cut green grass
The sky an old, familiar blue
Faded denim, just like your eyes
It reminds me how your face is familiar, too
Like something I've always known
Like something I've always had
Like something always meant to be mine
The tree we chose for shade today must be old as time
Mighty in its strength and perseverance
Oh, the things it has seen
I think of how our love feels powerful and ancient
Love knew us personally before we knew each other
It feels as if I was born to love you
I must have in another life, too
The wind dances softly around us
Invisible, moving force
Just like your love
It holds me in place and sets me free
Whirlwind of destiny
Consumed, I breathe in you

Tangled

My thoughts wander to the times
We would skip the event to head home and make love
We would touch just to be touching
Like it would be the last time we could
Our love was so fresh
Determined to prove the world wrong
Couldn't get enough
Flesh to flesh
Sex was like a self-discovery quest
I only knew myself when I was one with him
Lost with him
Tangled up in him
Tangled up in me
Undressed, my head on his chest
Our hearts talked all night
Making plans for the future
Bigger than us
Peace, quiet, candlelight
White wine
How could our love be so wrong?

Applause

He said a lot of things
I'm sweating
I'm not sure he knows what he means
His voice is barely audible, I'm sure his intentions are laudable
I wobble on my feet
Cobblestone streets
High gates
Heart races, I can't go home yet
I concentrate, but his words come back to set in
He must not know what he's doing
Only doing it because
I'm standing under the spotlight
He's waiting for the applause

Maria

She bats her long eyelashes
Black mascara
Her lipstick matte
Classic red
Full lips, the kind you crave to kiss
Does she know what trouble she causes?
Long dress, high split
To her hip
She enters a room
Hearts stop, conversation pauses
Fireworks boom
She's a cannon, dangerous but effective
A hundred men stand in line, but she's very selective
A hundred men fall in love with
Maria

Cinderella Dreams

I heard the faintest sound
A barely audible whisper
I had the inclination to look down
To see him fitting me with a glass slipper

My Layers

Spiritually
Intellectually
Mentally
Sexually
How many ways can a man get to me?
Into me
Into my head
Resurrect parts of me
Sworn off as long dead
I'm not afraid anymore
(Not like I was before)
How do you highlight
The way your willpower and fight waver?
It might fail
He's a man, not a savior
Layer by layer
He unravels my heart
Does the center hold
Or does it splinter apart?
The pieces land
Into his careful hands
Holds me close like contraband
This is only the very start
So I'm told

The Vanity

I stood nearly naked before the mirror
Drawing nearer to the edge of collapse
Dreadfully despise what I see
This reflection has me trapped
Pure vanity
I feel raw, vulnerable, aware
From the corner of my eye, I saw him standing there
Staring at my bareness
He's not seeing my imperfections
I elect to let him look, and he takes me in
The same as he took me then
I would burn this place to the ground
Yet he builds me up, as he holds me down
He takes me, slides into me, into destiny
He tastes his favorite flavor
Eyes wide open, whatever he sees must please
If only the damn vanity would return the favor

Outrun the sun

My confessions
Things I never told anyone
My sleeves are stained, but I hide them
I stood on the brink, now I'm flying
What do I have to give away?
Why do I have to?
My secrets to share
You don't have to care, why should you?
I'm just a poet with no name
What's been done can't be undone
I keep running
Trying to outrun the sun

Falling after all

If there's a chance
I take the first glance
Silence doesn't fill the room anymore
Your smile does
Whatever came before
Things I can't make sense of
We're here now because of
The person I choose to be now
Because of the lessons learned
Through hard kicks and growls
Your laughter is sheer innocence
It makes no sense how this makes sense
Here we are, falling
After all

Rise

It was no accident
The time we spent, we fell in love
No matter what, that was real
As time went on
We kept our heads above water
With fire at our feet
We couldn't change the outcome
I let go of the steering wheel
It's bittersweet
Do you regret what we've done
Or what we continue to do?
The wind sweeps and speaks in mysteries
"It's time to let go of me"
It tangles my insides
I don't know if it means me, or you?
So, I do the only thing I know how to do-
Rise.

He reaches in

How do you peel layers away
Without being invasive?
I'm a naysayer
I feel jagged and abrasive
I want to erase my past mistakes
Not take days to lay in the shame I give into
It's like he knew
Things move fast
Too fast
The way it is now
We move past first base
Suddenly, lose my head in the clouds
Down the rabbit hole I go
Heart racing
This wasn't my goal
I swear
He doesn't care, and I don't care
We're kissing and knock over the whiskey
It drenches me
I feel intensity, with emphasis in the right places
His face is light, free
His touch becomes necessity
I drown in serenity
Vision blurry, my senses leave me
But you don't, and won't, and can't imagine it

He believes in me
When it gets like this
I think my rough edges are too sharp to touch
He doesn't ask for much
Gives more than he takes
I hesitate, it takes practice
To avoid becoming distracted
With my own thoughts, my own pain
I relax, let the moment hang
He teaches me
As he reaches in to unpeel my layers
My clothes, and the emotions underneath

All of this, someday

I promise to learn you
Learn your ropes
Earn your trust
Bring to life your hopes
I promise not to run
I will learn to love
You and me both
I promise to follow where this goes
To dance in the sun
Not the shadows
I cherish your free spirit
And will always encourage your freedom
If I'm at your table, I don't care where I sit
When you say come, I come to your aid
I will praise the battles you've won
And shine your armor to remind you
Your worth on the days the scars hurt
And blind you
If you're lost, I promise to find you
I will watch you as you sleep
And keep the monsters at bay
I only hope you might promise me
All of this, too
Someday

Recover Me

You are your own entity
Incidentally, I've lost my identity
Fix me
Even accidentally
Recover me
In
Recovery
Complimentary characteristics
The language of love's linguistics
I'm not prepared mentally
Or physically
For the chemistry and brain activity
This brings up in me
It's frightening
Taking me to new heights to see the view
I don't know what you see in me
Only what I see in you

You, Only You

I fell in love with the idea of you
Not you for you
Inside I died for you
I've cried for you
Put aside my pride for you
I've glued my essence together
To weather what may come our way
To guide me
To guide you through the darkest days
Despite my indiscretions, imperfections
And predilections toward the obscene
Our hearts coincide
Swept away with the tide
It means nothing, and everything
To keep this keeping up with you
To stay true, and fight
All for the idea of you
I feel semiconscious
Wrestle with my conscience
What was once only me
Now only you
I see
I see only you
You, I only see you

This Moment

Blink, and you'll miss it
This chance we have
This kiss
This moment
Feel it
Feel me
All of me, all at once, everywhere
Everything
Every you and me we've dreamed
It's all happening
Here and now
Don't blink
We stand face to face
A firm stance
Our fingers laced
No second chance
We stand on the brink
Bringers of life, love, eternity
Eternally
We

Puppets

We dance
Keep dancing
Like puppets on a string
Never asking
About the important things
Masking
The pain
All the parts that sting
It's raining
Too numb to go inside
On each raindrop I'm wishing
Wash clean
Clean slate
Forgotten dreams
Reappear in blistering winds whisper
Yet I'm dancing
Like a puppet on a string
Never listening
To the important things

Pyre

Quiet prayers
Said under sparkling stars
Around the bright, billowing bonfire
Finding miracles in night's desire
I lay my regrets on the pyre
Dance to the rhythm of the Source
I feel the flaming heat deep in my core
Burning out the unnecessary
The unyielding
This is my reclaiming
Clearing space, allowing for more
Breathing room for healing

Holy Chokehold

I once turned to dark sky
To ask why, and cry
With no ready, righteous reply
Only quiet, empty, endless nights greeted me
My heart beats, but badly broken
I have unfinished business
In diminished dimensions
A token of my mind's inventions
Of age-old superstitions
And wishes that don't turn to gold
I buckle under the pressure
Fold under the stressors
Put under a holy chokehold

Mind's Bent

My heart's become a barren land
Cracked open, spills sand
Movement from the arteries
Each beat
Spent eternities
Mind's bent, I ease into the resistance
Consistency
Releases me from my reveries

Shattered Time (Haiku)

Time calls me by name
Whispers finite promises
The hourglass flips now

Closeted Chaos

I lovingly let you in
You suddenly shut me out
You, me
Meet in between
Devils dancing in the dark
We are what we mean to be
Hardened hearts
Meant to be
Desperately
Cling to closeted chaos
All is not lost
We are just frost in the night
At first light, we thaw

December Snow

My eyes met the moonlit snow
Through the window
Before first light
Cold and eyes wide
I get up and go outside
To absorb the majestic quiet

Silence

Listen, as silence steals the atmosphere
Dark eyelashes wet from trickling tears
Evidence of failure to beat back emotion
I feel. (Everything.)
A soft sniffle here and there
The moon a singular witness to this ordeal
Pale and far away it seems
An unbiased judge
I see forever in its surface
Wonder what my purpose is
Here, in another moment borrowed
The night air caresses my face
Kisses me like a dreary, distant dream
I wait for the silence to still my heartbeat
Fast, slow, slower, into tranquility
As today slowly circles into tomorrow

Dare to be immortal?

Do we dare to be immortal?
Taste it just to see
Taste a tiny morsel
Of sweet infinity
When forever delicately dances
On the tip of the tongue
To the tune of time's tempo
Eons unsung
Expanding expanses
If only time were just a portal
Would we take the chance of chances
And dare to be immortal?

She's a real poet!

My god, I'm inspired!

She says everything I want to say and says it better.

With a passion and real fire

that comes from carefully crafted chaos, and real loss, and a culmination of heartbreak and hot takes, and a soapbox to stand on.

I want to say things that pretty. I want people to get me.

I want to shout from the rooftops my own loss, I want my own box, and remind myself who the hell I am. But damn.

Sometimes, memories aren't to be revisited, and sometimes I find emotions that do not equal the vocabulary I have that's limited. An implosion is imminent, isn't it?

I want to emulate the greatness I see, but all I can be is me, and let others resonate with my beautiful simplicity.

Dancing Daggers

Desperate to reinvent
Shed skin
Feel blood rush again
In my head
Daggers are dancing
Laughter is menacing
I implore, explore
But I can't tell the difference anymore
Anything new seems fancy

Three words and silence

The words sit at the tip of my tongue
Like a forgotten ballad gone unsung
I wait to speak, a pause because
My heart's too weak, this love's too young
My silent response could break his spirit
To say only once, begs not to hear it
He said, "I love you," my voice runs dry
I would reply, I miss my cue
I have no choice
My tongue is tied, I feel unsteady
Silence hung as I'm not ready
To vocalize I love him, too

It's okay, I like chaos

Blurred lines are not indicative to what we're really after
What divides us is infinitely bigger than mixed signals and marked palms
You've mastered the art of smooth talk
Past pool tables and drunk laughter
I've perfected the art of pretending to give a damn
The light falls on your face just right
With that smile to die for
I wonder what goes on in that head of yours
I think of colliding trains and hurricanes
Destruction, disaster
It looks beautiful behind blue eyes
I've always liked chaos, so it's okay

Deity to me

Freshly showered, looked like a Greek god in a towel
Enough to make a woman pray for redemption
From the very thoughts I was thinking
Was I supposed to divert my eyes?
Below my waistline howls
Aching, pulsing sensation
I feel playful
Empowered
I'm not a saint, nor exempt from temptation
His coy smile told me our thoughts were parallel
A short struggle with my pride, suddenly
It's like I'm in someone else's skin
I'm doing things with him that must be illegal somewhere
But not here, and not now
The bedside table lamp casts our shadow on the wall
They melt and blend together, unable to define what's him Or what's me
It's only us, and forward thrusts into ecstasy
"Oh my god"
Is he my god? He is to me, deity

Dodging Bullets

I was mesmerized
Blindsided
Can I truly claim naivety?
I had myself an old-fashioned
Self-absorbed tantrum turned pity party
I cried and I cried
Because what we had was passion
But every time "we" would gain traction
This stupid motherfucker lied
I don't know if he thinks I'm slow to catch on, or dense
I'm just smart enough to know when things don't add up
Or make sense
I know I dodged a bullet dodging him
And I know I'll be alright
Just can't say when

The weight of expectations

Why can't I love myself?
Shrug the expectations off
A certain weight, a certain firmness
I stare at myself in earnest
Hate what I see in the mirror
I want to be near her, love her
But she is too soft here, too big there
I run my fingers through tangled hair
Dark circles, I can't bear it anymore
Throw up what I ate before
Sick with myself
Quickly lock, then slide against the door
And remember to love myself some more

Take Notes

Whatever you get from me, intellectually
Through my poetry
It isn't me, just my ability
To turn thoughts into words
To say in colorful ways
All of the ways it hurts
Existence into writing
Pretty and petite
I try not to repeat myself
It's frightening
Diving so deep into my soul
Exposing my desires and hopes
But it's not me that does the writing
It's my heart, I just take notes

Clearly

In the vodka nothing
The clear abyss
Liquid shifts
Flexible
Accessible
Into nothing & everything I drown
A stout kiss to the lips, and I see heaven now

Gray

Shattered fragments of reality
Silhouettes in gray shades of yesterdays
Something dies inside of me
I stood in the icy rain, pounding at the air
Insane
Gasping for breath
Drowning
All that mattered is a memory now
I'll learn to be okay

Starving

I hear my stomach growl
A satisfaction settles in
How many days has it been?
Midnight kitchen prowl
I don't have an appetite
(Only a few more pounds 'til I'm "thin")
Leave empty-handed with a scowl
A million things I can't control
I can control this
Even though
When I don't eat, it eats my soul
So many layers to unpeel
All I know is
It doesn't taste as good as skinny feels

Acronyms

Are we mirroring, or am I projecting again?
I'm so acclimated to dysfunction, maybe neither
Is it my ADHD or RSD
Or some other psychological acronym?
We're revisiting conversations we've had
Countless times before now
The click, click, click of my acrylics
Impatience
My boredom always gets me into trouble
Somehow
Hurling myself headfirst at anything that gives me
Any semblance of happy brain chemicals
Or relief
"I didn't mean to" doesn't mean shit
I refuse to drown others so I can breathe
That's what makes us different

Truth Speaks

Withering into nothing
My heart is a wilderness
Wild and wailing
Emotions at a stalemate
One foot forward
I'm falling apart at the seams
The floorboard creaks
An exhausted, futile groan
My heaven, hell, and heartbreak
The truth speaks
This house is not a home

Six

This charade shakes my subconscious
Shattered shades of blue
Champagne sips, sultry silk
I slip out of my slip and onto your lips
My racing heart reverberates against my upright spine
We tip-toe the line
My body's yours, yours is mine
We might manage to fuck the feelings away in time
The old adage
"Out of sight, out of mind"
I wade through the muck only to find
My heart damaged
And I've been blind
We move too fast
Then cold, then hot
We are, then not
Whiplash and distraught
Six tingling tastes of sideways sublime

Hard vs. Harder

The hard best thing
And the harder right thing
Brazenly brawled inside my heart
The fight was over what I wanted
Versus what I needed
Neither thing was easy
Tiptoe quietly in the dark
Afraid to startle you, or wake you
I pack my things quietly
I pray you know I don't hate you

Trellis

I took a second look
Into the night
From my window
All I make out is an ethereal glow from a low moon
On a trellis of vines
Covered in dew
Mocking me
Because they grow
Fast and fierce
With little to no attention
While I'm hanging in suspension
Rocking
In a corner of my mind
Tracing dotted lines
With a red pen
In a children's book
When did I begin to envy ivy?
I ricochet off every emotion inside of me
Lie with me
Lie to me
Tell me that
The flowers in my garden are fragrant
Tell me that
My closets are vacant
The monsters have all died

The ghosts found peace
Half past midnight
The fireplace offers both warmth and light
Although, in this dire state, I feel neither

Illumination

The light in you
Shines brightly on me
It pours through your cracks
Illuminating both the good and bad
In us both
The way you hold yourself together
Despite it all
Your head held high
Embracing your flaws
I love your positivity
And radiance
Your smile lights up a hundred-mile radius
You complete me, completely
The light in you
Forever
Shines brightly on me

A nook and a book

You were never one to look around much, or ask questions
My curiosity roars, yours is only implied
That style of ignorance drives me insane
I hear your thoughts echo from the void space in your brain
Attractive, but plain
I want to know the who, the when, the why to life
I'll know the where when I get there
(If I ever arrive)
You are content to just be alive, dull and blind
Pull the wool from my eyes, let me see clearly
The eerie, quiet knowledge embraces me
Like a long-lost lover's kiss
I feel warmth through the dreariness
And I know, there's something more
I'm transfixed
Give me a nook and a book
Let me die like this
In comprehension's bliss
Not in cognitive dissonance

Chaos Pt. 2

Just a touch
A taste
A shadow of my courage
My first instinct is to hesitate
I see the silhouette of a brave woman
My reflection displays a coward
I move three steps forward
Only to fall two behind
Sixteen years I've waited to have this life
Stability, my semblance of happiness
If it isn't wrecked, I grow bored
Chaos and loss
And nonstop, blackout fights
Long nights
Bitter regrets
Objects of far-fetched fascination
Why am I like this?
It's my fault, not his
Me and my darkened imagination

Release Me

I wanted to let go
You wouldn't let me
I cried mercy and I begged
Release me
How can we dissolve our ties and disconnect?
I lay my offering at your feet
I've said please
I've sacrificed my own identity
Forgotten what makes me, me
It's hard to surrender something
You've held onto tightly for so long
I know it's hard to see it end here
Neither one of us belonged here
We both deserve to breathe free
Even if initially, it isn't easy
We've bounced to and fro
Dancing in the wind
It's time to let go
Stop trying to pretend
You've never been the one
Not now, and not then

A blip on the radar

I can't keep living as if tomorrow is a guarantee
At 33, I've already lost too many friends who met their ends too soon
They all had one thing in common
They all had plans for the next day
The old cliché'
"Every moment is a gift"
It really is
Life is just a blip
On the radar
In the grand scheme of the universe

One more time

What would unfold
If I called you one more time?
It's been a while
Are we strangers now?
Unable to speak our minds
A one-night stand
Turned into three
After dark the city glows
There are secrets I keep
Only you know
I barely remember getting home
Memories creep
And I know my weakness
But I erased your number from my phone

The intensity (Haiku)

Intensity flows
Radiates down my cold spine
Can you handle it?

Wish

Wish for emotions that leaned on the positive side
I experience deeply, I always have
Intensity followed my heels my whole life
I focus my perception on the bright side
The silver lining
Watch for a break in the clouds
Wish for a white knight
Wish for the spotlight
I've gone broke from the wishing well
Hot blooded passion
Blistering in my own hell

La Fin

Thank You!

Special thanks to the following people (in no particular order) for their unwavering love and support.

Brent E.

Angie E.

Dean F.

Tori J.

Gary W.

Dejai F.

Eric M.

David T.

Melanie B.

Deb S.

My entire Twitter family (you know who you are!)

Thank you for believing in me and filling my cup to the brim. Thank you for the pep talks, opinions on how a poem sounds, sharing your own work with me, and for hyping me up when I forget who the hell I am.

You are just as much a part of this work as I am.

I love you all.

-W